# DATE DUE

|  |  |  |  |
|--|--|--|--|
|  |  |  |  |
|  |  |  |  |
|  |  |  |  |
|  |  |  |  |
|  |  |  |  |
|  |  |  |  |
|  |  |  |  |
|  |  |  |  |
|  |  |  |  |
|  |  |  |  |
|  |  |  |  |
|  |  |  |  |
|  |  |  |  |

# Home Safety

by Peggy Pancella

Heinemann Library
Chicago, Illinois

© 2005 Heinemann Library,
a division of Reed Elsevier Inc.
Chicago, Illinois

Customer Service 888-454-2279
Visit our website at www.heinemannlibrary.com

Designed by Heinemann Library
Page layout by Roslyn Broder
Printed and bound in China by South China Printing Co. Ltd.

09 08 07 06 05
10 9 8 7 6 5 4 3 2 1

**Library of Congress Cataloging-in-Publication Data**
Pancella, Peggy.
  Home safety / Peggy Pancella.
      v. cm. -- (Be safe!)
  Includes bibliographical references and index.
  Contents: What is safety? -- Getting around safely -- Kitchen safety -- Sharp objects -- Bathroom safety -- Poisons -- Choking -- Electricity -- Fire safety -- Computer safety -- Home alone-- Safety around guns-- Make a safety plan -- Safety tips.
  ISBN 1-4034-4932-5 (hard) -- ISBN 1-4034-4941-4 (pbk.)
  1. Home accidents--Prevention--Juvenile literature. [1. Dwellings--Safety measures. 2. Safety.] I. Title.
  HV675.5.P357 2004
  613.6--dc22

                                2003024064

**Acknowledgments**
The author and publisher are grateful to the following for permission to reproduce copyright material:
Cover photograph by Corbis
p. 4 Corbis; pp. 5, 15, 17, 20 David Young-Wolff/Photo Edit, Inc.; p. 6 Myrleen Ferguson Cate/Photo Edit, Inc.; p. 7 Royalty-free-Corbis; pp. 8, 21, 25, 28 Robert Lifson/Heinemann Library; p. 9 Tony Freeman/Photo Edit, Inc.; pp. 10, 13 Warling Studios/Heinemann Library; p. 11 Michael Keller/Corbis; p. 12 Barbara Stitzer/Photo Edit, Inc.; p. 14 Dana White/Photo Edit, Inc.; pp. 16, 18, 22 Michael Newman/Photo Edit, Inc.; p. 19 Spencer Grant/Photo Edit, Inc.; p. 23 Bill Aron/Photo Edit, Inc.; pp. 24, 29 Jonathan Nourok/Photo Edit, Inc.; p. 26 Jim Oltersdorf Outdoor Photography/www.joltersdorf.com; p. 27 Alastair Cardwell Photography

Every effort has been made to contact copyright holders of any material reproduced in this book. Any omissions will be rectified in subsequent printings if notice is given to the publisher.

# Contents

Some words are shown in bold, **like this.** You can find out what they mean by looking in the glossary.

# What Is Safety?

It is important for everyone to stay safe.
Being safe means keeping out of danger.
It means staying away from things or
people that could hurt you.

Safety is important in everything you do. One good place to be safe is at home. You do many different things where you live. Learning some rules to follow at home can help you stay safe.

# Getting Around Safely

When you move through your house, walk instead of running. Hold the railing when you use the stairs. Also, pick up toys from the floor so no one trips and falls.

If you cannot reach something, ask an adult for help. Never climb on furniture, boxes, or other objects to reach something high. A fall could hurt you.

# Kitchen Safety

Working in the kitchen is fun, but many things can be dangerous. Always have an adult help you. Be careful when you are near ovens or stoves. Use oven mitts and pads to handle hot things.

Wash up before you eat or handle food. Clean fruits and vegetables before eating them. Keep cold foods cold and read the **labels** to see how long foods will stay fresh. Do not eat anything that looks or smells rotten.

# Sharp Objects

Many things in your home are sharp enough to cut you. Let adults use knives and other sharp tools. Handle scissors, pencils, and other sharp or pointy objects carefully.

When something breaks, ask an adult to sweep up the pieces and throw them away. If you do get cut, clean up with soap and water. Then cover the cut with a bandage.

# Bathroom Safety

Many **accidents** happen in bathrooms. Puddles can be slippery, so wipe up spilled water right away. If you use a rug or floor mat, get one that does not slip around.

Wash your hands after using the toilet.
Make sure the water does not get too hot!
Check bath water before getting in, too.
A mat in the tub can keep you from
slipping and falling.

# Poisons

Most homes have containers of dangerous **poisons,** such as cleaners and bug sprays. Only adults should handle these. Do not touch, smell, or taste anything unless you are sure it is food.

Not all poisons look the same. Never take medicines yourself. Only a trusted adult should give you medicine.

# Choking

You may choke on small things that get caught in your throat. Chew your food well, and never run with food in your mouth. Do not put toys in your mouth, either.

Other things may stop you from breathing, too. Never wrap anything tightly around your neck. Do not play with cords, strings, or plastic bags. Keep them away from babies and pets, too.

# Electricity

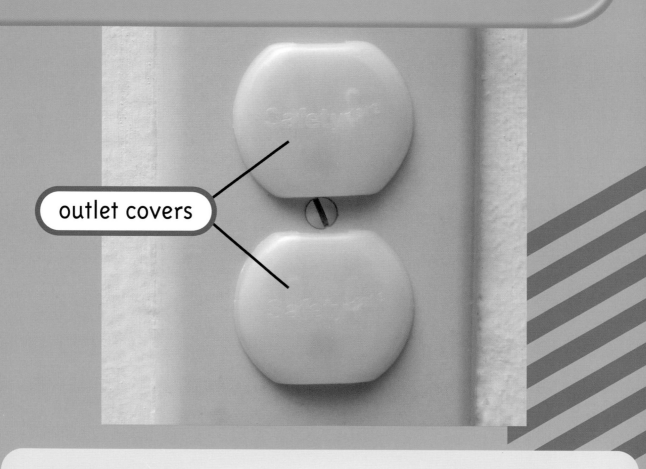

outlet covers

**Electricity** gives us power, but it is very dangerous. Never touch an **outlet,** and cover any outlets that are not being used. Only adults should plug in and handle electrical **appliances.**

Water and electricity are very unsafe together. Always dry your hands before touching anything that has electric power. Never use electrical appliances near a sink or bathtub.

# Fire Safety

We use fire for cooking, heating, and light, but it can be dangerous, too. Never play with matches, lighters, candles, heaters, or other objects that could start fires.

**Smoke detectors** can warn you when there is a fire. Make and practice a fire escape plan with your family. This will help you be ready if there is a real fire.

# Computer Safety

It is fun to play computer games and send **e-mail** to friends. But you may find things **online** that seem strange or scary. Always ask an adult before using the computer.

When you are online, never give your whole name, address, phone number, or **password** to anyone. Tell an adult if people ask you **personal** questions or if anything makes you feel **uncomfortable.**

# Home Alone

Family Numbers

| | |
|---|---|
| Emergency | 911 |
| Sheriff | 555-0011 |
| Family Doctor | 555-3482 |
| Dentist | 555-4323 |
| Optometrist | 555-0984 |
| Dad's Work | 555-4932 |
| School | 555-3695 |
| Grandma Ann | 555-2904 |

If you are ever home alone, lock the doors. If anyone calls, do not say you are alone. You can say your parents are napping or taking a shower. A small lie is okay to stay safe.

Never open the door for anyone—even for people you know or think you can trust. Ask them to come back later. If they do not leave, call a trusted neighbor or dial **911**.

# Safety Around Guns

Some families keep guns in their homes. Real guns can look like toy guns, but they are much more dangerous. Never touch a gun or point it at anyone.

Guns should be kept in a locked drawer or cabinet. If you find a gun, or if someone is holding one, leave the room. Tell an adult right away.

# Make a Safety Plan

Your family can make a plan for staying safe. Think of problems that might happen. Then decide how to handle the problems. You can act out what you will do.

Make an **emergency** phone list. Write numbers for your parents at work, and for the police, firefighters, doctor, and trusted neighbors. Hang a list near each telephone in your house.

# Family Numbers

| Emergency | 911 |
|---|---|
| Sheriff | 555-0011 |
| Family Doctor | 555-3482 |
| Dentist | 555-4323 |
| Optometrist | 555-0984 |
| Dad's Work | 555-4932 |
| School | 555-3695 |
| Grandma Ann | 555-2904 |

# Safety Tips

- Walk in your home and on the stairs.

- Clean up toys and spills so no one falls.

- Ask an adult to help you with things that are hot, sharp, dangerous, or too high to reach.

- Make safety plans so you will know how to handle problems when they happen.

- Hang a list of **emergency** numbers near every telephone.

# Glossary

**911** phone number to dial in an emergency

**accident** something that happens unexpectedly

**appliance** piece of household equipment

**electricity** natural force that provides power

**e-mail** message sent from one computer to another

**emergency** unexpected event

**label** sticker or tag that gives information about something you buy

**online** computer connected to a main computer

**outlet** place to plug an electrical cord to get power

**password** word you use to read and send emails

**personal** about a certain person; private

**poison** dangerous substance that can hurt or kill you

**smoke detector** fire alarm that goes off when it senses smoke

**uncomfortable** feeling like something is wrong

# Index